Kaleidoscope

A Collection

Pam Collings

Published by Pam Collings

Copyright © Pam Collings 2012

Cataloguing-in-Publication Data
available from the National Library of Australia

Collings, Pam
Kaleidoscope

ISBN 978-0-9871238-3-1 (pbk)

All rights reserved. No part of this publication
may be reproduced, stored in a retrieval system,
or transmitted, in any form, by any means,
electronic, mechanical, photocopying, recording
or otherwise, without prior permission from the author.

Typeset in Footlight MT Light 13 pt

Produced by **TB Books**
 P.O. Box 556
 Wallan Victoria 3756
 Email: info@tbbooks.com.au

Contents

Introduction 7
Déjà vu 9
Me, Myself, I 10
Out of the Mists 12
Resolution 14
Sands in the Hourglass 16
Confusion 18
The Pen in the Pot 20
Onward 22
My Glasses and me 24
In All Good Time 26
Silver Threads 29
Consequences 30
Movement 32
Soft Book Covers 34
Finding the Unicorn 37
Dust 41
Beyond 44
The Slide 46
No Idea! 48

Missing you	51
Memory	52
Little Miss Harpy	54
The Hated One	56
Corners of Time	58
Monster Tub	59
The Bearmaker	62
Today's World	67
Beyond the Window	70
Inside My Mind	72
Strange Encounter	74
Revisiting	76
The Luck of Destiny	79
Peace Regained	80
Invisible	82
Rainbow of Life	84
Spirit Guide	86
Waiting	88
Snowballs	90
Mystery	92
Caught Between Hope and Fear	94
The Funniest Thing	96
Accidental Knowledge	99

Beginning	100
My Favourite Martian	102
Believe It or Not	104
Blue Bird Fly Free	106
The Mystery of the Missing Daphne	108
Toothache	111
Mistaken	112
Make of This What You Will	114
Magical Moment	116
Where I'd like to Be	118
My Scarecrow	120
Haiku Trio	122
Wants, Needs, Wishes	125
Reality	128
Visions of Family	130
The Author	135

Introduction

I never planned to be a poet; always saw myself writing fantasy, more than anything else.

But when I was in Form 6, I found I needed something to relieve the stress. I was already writing heaps of prose stuff and reading like it was going out of fashion, so neither of these usual stress-relieving activities were helping.

One day I sat down and looked around my bedroom and decided to write a poem about what I saw. So I spent the next half hour dashing down a poem about a hat, I believe (somehow it's got lost).

When I finally looked up from my pad I felt like a huge stone had rolled off my shoulders. It's worked for me ever since.

Poetry, for me, is a very personal form of writing and is all about the feelings. There's no hidden meaning in my words, at least, none that I know about, but I do try to portray some kind of feeling.

This book is an even more personal and exciting thing, as it is the event that will take me from being unpublished to published, from being a writer to an author. And not just an ordinary author, either, but a poet, someone who truly sees the world through the words of creation. Someone who creates music with these words, which hopefully sing to those who read them.

Even if you are not into poetry, I'd like to think that there is something in these pages for everyone to enjoy and hum to.

Thank you for reading!

Déjà vu

At times
I've been here before,
Most times
Everything's new.

Last time,
I took a step
And the familiar
Wrapped around me.

That time,
It made me
Feel warm and safe,
But it doesn't always.

Meantime,
When nothing
Is familiar,
I wish I'd been here before.

Sometimes,
But not always,
I have been here before,
Or maybe I just think so.

Me, Myself, I

Thicker
And tougher
Than armour.

Crushing
And squeezing
To death.

Breathless
And frightened
To live.

Cowered
And timid
Each day.

Thinking
And feeling
It's real.

Despairing,
Depressed in
This life.

Then ...

Stronger
And harder
The will.

Survival
And life
To fulfil.

Layers
And layers
Fall off.

Time
And effort
Must win.

To make me
What
I can be.

Nothing more,
Nothing less,
I'm agreed.

It's for me now,
For me,
And my dreams.

Out of the Mists

Around the corner,
And up the hill,
An idea lies in wait

For someone to come near.

Footsteps tread a path,
A second time around
Knowing where they've been,

Skipping lightly by.

In the distance of the day,
The shadow waves and beckons.
It waits as one draws near.

It knows where it must go.

The heart warms to one,
Unknown, unlikely,
As the day fades.

A hand reaches out.

The road branches,
Leaving one to form three,

The feet reach the intersection.

They turn towards the light.

A helping hand,
A beacon bright,
A pull this way or that,
A thought of right,
A warmness,
A longing.

The mists part,
To move on,
To explore,
To experience,
To live

Where facts have no room.

Resolution

New Year's Eve,
A time to change,
When fear creeps in,
When hope comes to visit.

The cries of the New Year
Ring out loud and healthy,
Pyrotechnic smoke
Odouring the air.

It is a time of beginnings,
A time of endings,
A time of grief
For what could have been.

A time of pleasure
For what may be.

The champagne glasses
Raise their half full,
Half empty crystalline forms
Bright within the contents.

Dull and lifeless elsewhere.

Resolutions uttered.

Fill hearts with wonder
As the bright lights rain
Down upon ecstatic heads.

For some the year ahead
Would bring relief
As they move into a good year.

For others the year
Will be filled with unwanted
Unlucky badness,
Or despair.

The bad one will pass,
Like all things,
It is necessary
To appreciate the good ones.

The bad have their purpose,
The bad are good,
Resolutions are spoken,
And sometimes they are kept.

Everything always changes.

Sands in the Hourglass

Watch the time
Tick away
On the clock.

Hands move
Slowly, irrevocably
From one beat to the next.

Numbers move
Rhythmically, surely,
Growing ever larger.

Breathe in,
Breathe out,
Eye lashes blinking.

Mind rolls on
Weaving in and out
Of a myriad of thoughts.

Thoughts quiver
Through limbs,
Digits tapping

In time with
The ticking

Of the clock.

The sands in the hourglass of futility.

Confusion

Not worth it,
What do you mean?

What have I done?

Why are you doing this?

Bastard.

Heavy and grey,
No lights on the horizon,
Heart weighing 200 kilos,
In an 80 kilo body.

Tear escapes,
Trickles along the pores,
Runs down the cheeks,

Splashes on the desk.

It spreads,
Breaks up,
Dries up.

Empty – for a while.

Chin lifts,
Shafts of sunlight
Shoot through the gloom.

Bury the pain.

Life recovers.

Smile defeats confusion.

The Pen in the Pot

It's useful, you know
The pen in the pot

But ever so often
The pen it is not.

It scurries here
And it scurries there
And when you need it
You know not where.

For the pen in the pot
Has a mind of its own
And it does not like
To wait by the phone.

It would rather be used
To make sounds like a drum
Especially when you need
To upset your Mum.

Or better still
It loves to hop
Beside someone's ear
So it's near to the top.

It loves to travel
From here to there
As it wobbles on top
It can go anywhere.

So no wonder the pen
Never sits in its pot
Waiting and waiting
A lot and a lot.

Onward

Bright points
Of light
March off
Into the distance.

Hypnotic
Thoughts float
Unbidden
In a lost mind.

The distance
Marches off
Into a future
Of uncertainty.

Only time
Knows what
Lies ahead
On that dark road.

Sometimes
The foot
Eagerly
Presses forward.

But then

No!
It eases
Almost to a stop.

Concentration wanes
On the onward
Track.

Carelessness prevails.

My Glasses and me

Tell me, glasses,
When did I begin to age?
I don't feel any different,
Just a bit blurry on the page.

As I twirl you, glasses,
In my hands of shaky kind,
Soft mist swirls of yesterday,
Appear in my over-tired mind.

Glasses, wait a minute,
You're needed for my mission,
I rise to greet my aches and pains,
As the floor twitches with a vision.

Glasses, can you see it, too?
My friend so newly gotten,
The rainbow colours of my life,
Surround all that I've forgotten.

I need you now, I think you know,
I think you think you do,
You hang upon my crooked nose,
Amidst sweat that's just like glue,

Where are you, glasses?

Damn you, time, damn you every day,
As I tremble in the aftermath,
Of a lifetime streaked with grey.

Oh, there you are, my seeing friend,
Hanging beneath my double chin,
Now exactly what did I need to see?

Oh, right, the courage and hope I hold within.

In All Good Time

Time to think,
Time to lean back and relax,
To learn what needs to be learned,
That's what I need.

Just time.
Money would be good, too.
But time most of all,
When silence can spill

Through the cracks,
And seep round the edges,
And silence
Can seek out the quiet

Inner recesses
That have become
Lost and barren.

Silence and time.

To spell the truth
Of existence,
To let the essence
Of creation

Scent the very air
And thoughts I breathe
So that no-one
Can destroy the me

That is growing
And becoming what
It needs to be.

So that the I that is me
Has time and peace
To spread and blossom
And *be* all that I can be

In the silence and the time and the peace.

Just to be me.

No strings attached.
No responsibilities.
No hang-ups.

Just all confidence,
And joy,
And hope,
And contentment.

Embracing life,

Living life,
Until my heart is full
And my mind is complete.

Until the me that I am
Is here amongst the silence
And the peace.

In all good time.

That's what I want – what I need.

Silver Threads

Silver threads
Wind
Round and round
In perfect harmony

Dew drops
Cling minutely
To fine
Thread

Mist drifts
By
Wafting
Through sunshine

The dazzling
Yellow glow
Startles
As it comes

This
Is
Morning

Consequences

Bubbles hit the surface,
Break,
And travel in circles
Away
From the point of their birth.

Air spreads out around,
Away,
From the moving object
Breathing,
In a rush of anticipation.

Buds grow on branches,
Spreading,
Upwards towards the sun,
Warming
Them until they unfurl.

Spatters of rain,
Fall,
Upon parched earth,
Sleeping,
Grass seeds waken and stretch.

Angry words spew from lips,
Untouched,

Angry images bombard ears,
Oblivious
To emotions in an empty heart.
Life performs feats of wonder,
Around
Lives no longer lived,
Striving
To repair the mosaic of a story.

A story,
Written with an untimely ending,
The reader,
Left dissatisfied.

Movement

Bleached bones
Sightless sockets
Stare out
From stillness.

Once shrouded
In entrails
Muscles and fat
Held together with hide.

Amidst the rocks
The transparent slithering
Lies comatose
And brittle.

The entity
Once adorned
By the intricate shell
Long gone into the shade.

Hanging from a tree
An empty husk
Abandoned
Its duty performed.

Have swept the new kind

Far beyond the horizon
To an unknown destiny.

A cry sings out
The tapping of little feet follow
Shouts of play ring true
Tuneless singing from headphoned ears.

Time pushes skills into overcrowded minds
Church bells peel, confetti rains,
Little feet tap, little voices laugh, pride swells,
Rooms empty and fill with silence.

Peaceful sighs and wrinkled smiles
Give way to empty sadness
Eyes close, chest stills,
Hands grow cold.

The tombstone is raised,
A tear is shed,
A little hand clasped in one much larger,
A tiny smile warms the grief.

A cry sings out
And the tapping of little feet
Lead to shouting play,
And the day moves on.

Soft Book Covers

'Okay, Johnny. Grandma
Will just be here reading.
You go off and play.'

Their eyes clashed and
Rita found her heart beating
A fast tango.

'Grandma – look at me.'

'That's nice, dear.'
He held her in his arms.
They were almost one.
Their lips melted together
And she thought she would die.

'Grandma – I can see so much
from here. You should look.'

'Yes, dear, that's nice, dear.'

Bare skin touched bare skin,
But the contact was still not
Close enough.
She longed to feel him
Thrust deep within her.

A moan of anticipation ...

'Grandma! Grandma!'
'Yes, dear.'

... escaped her lips,
Their bodies glistened in the
half light,
Time stood still.
He raised himself
And hovered for an
Eternity above her.
Slowly he lowered
Himself.
She felt his manhood swollen
and urgent between her legs.
Would he never relieve her need?

'Grandma! Grandma!
I'm slipping!
Help!'

'Yes, dear.'
'Please Grandma,
I'm in trouble.'

Unfocused eyes,

Dangling body,

Fingernails gripping,
Sigh of resignation,
Exclamation of relief.

Gasps of passion,
Hidden for now,
Between soft book covers.

Finding the Unicorn

Everyone says unicorns don't exist,
Well, *I* know they do.
Because my best friend is a unicorn.

I'm pretty much an expert on unicorns,
You know,
I've read just about everything
Ever written about them.

But everyone always talks
About unicorns in Europe,
Or Britain,
Or even America.

So *I* thought,
What about Australia?

I decided that Australia
Was the only place
Unicorns would live.

And I set out to prove it.

But Mum and Dad
Wouldn't let me go very far
Exploring for them.

So I'm very lucky
That my unicorn lives nearby.

The first day I saw him,
I could hardly believe my eyes.

I'd decided to explore,
In the bush behind my house,
I went off through
The rough, almost impassable
Bushes.

I had to fight my way through.

I got all scratched
And ripped my jumper,
And was making lots of noise,
So I thought I'd never find one.

Then up ahead of me,
In a small clearing,
Right in the middle,
Was the most beautiful
Creature I'd ever seen.

His coat was pure white,
Covered with flecks of silver

That glittered in the bright sunlight.

His golden horn gleamed,
He looked peaceful and happy.

I stumbled out,
But he took no notice of me,
Not until I was almost touching him.

Then he shied and reared into the air.
It was then that I saw his hooves
Were made of crystal.

I screamed
Because I thought he'd rip me to pieces.
He screamed, but let his hooves drop to earth.

And then he spoke.
It was beautiful, but VERY, VERY loud.

You see. the poor thing is hard of hearing.

We've been friends ever since.

But just a bit of friendly advice.

If you come across a unicorn
In the bush.

Make lots of noise

So they hear you coming.
If not, you'll startle them,
And they'll disappear.

Dust

It floats on the breeze,
It hovers in the sunshine,
It makes you sneeze,
It lives.

It comes when you least
Want it,
To settle on that painting
You've just finished.

Or delicately alight
Upon your polished
Tabletops,
Moments after you've shined them.

Its colour is indeterminate,
Or maybe it just changes,
Because painting in dust colour
Doesn't seem to help.

If you paint grey,
Then it comes up brown,
If you paint brown,
It comes out grey.

And let's not speak

About other colours.

But where does it come from?
What has it seen?
Who might it be?
Should we really clean it away?

What if it's Aunt Mable come to stay?
Or 2000 years down the track
What if it's Jesus Christ?
Would we go to hell

For Mr Sheening our tabletop or TV,
Wiping up JC with our cloth
And throwing it in the bin?

Perhaps not,
But I think,
From now on,
I'll play it safe
And leave well enough
Alone.

When you visit,
You might like to bring
Your hayfever medicine,
And please don't wipe

Any hard surfaces,
You never know
Who you might be disturbing.

Hope to see you soon!

Beyond

Others live out there,
Somewhere,
Amongst the multitude,
Of stars.

Somewhere,
In that dark expanse,
Sewn with glittering,
Worlds

There lies another,
World, maybe more,
Where other people,
Play

And gaze
Back through
The black expanse
Of space.

And wonder
How many other
Worlds
There are.

While we gaze

Up and out
And see no one
Else.

But try to grasp
The fact
That we may be
The only life

To exist
In thousands of billions
Of possible
Habitats.

The only life
Intent on making
The universe
Barren.

The only life
Intent on
Destruction.

Have a great day!

The Slide

All the way up,
So high, so high,
I surely must be
Almost at the sky.

One step, two,
I hold on tight,
This had just better
Be worth the fight.

Breath so short,
Hammering heart,
It's been so long,
Since I left the start.

At last the top
Is within my reach.
Too late, I look down
And let out a screech.

I settle myself,
On the very top seat,
Close my eyes,
And point my feet.

A gentle push,

And I'm on my way.
I close my eyes,
And quietly pray.

The wind is cold
As I speed my way down,
And I hit the bottom,
Making me frown.

I forgot to brake
So I did not stop,
As I slid very fast,
Down from the top.

The damage is done,
And my right hand is hurt,
But not a drop of blood,
Did my right hand spurt.

I hold my tears,
And try to be brave,
Even when my sister,
Has her angry rave.

My day on the big slide,
Has come to an end,
I must make my way home,
With my sister and friend.

No Idea!

Mind open,
Come on
Flock to me,
Ideas.

Wait –
Nothing –
Black abyss,
No light at the end.

Clock ticks
Tocks
Pens scratch
Light beats down.

Ideas.
What are they?
I ask.
But no answer.

Silence,
Sighs falling
Deeply
Into the dark hole.

Time
Marching onwards,
Waiting for
Ideas.

But –
There are none,
Not a one.
Not a jot.

Flown
Out the doors
And windows
Of my empty

Mind
That wants to know
Why
Do I need

An idea
At all.
It's a joke,
Surely a joke.

But even a joke
Has an idea
And I don't.
Not a one.

No idea!

Missing you

Where have you gone?
Where are you now?
I miss you now
That you have gone.

I look in your eyes.
They're the same,
Almost, yet,
They've changed.

You talk to me,
But there is nothing said,
You sound,
Different ... younger ... innocent.

But still there lingers
Touches of you,
The bitterness you feel,
The hatred you hold.

I wish I could
Talk to you,
Like I used to,
Like I need to.

I miss the way you were.

Memory

He rests
His hands
Upon the wooden
Rail

Gazes lovingly
Into the baby's
Innocent eyes,
And sighs.

He reaches
Down
And strokes
The soft cheeks.

'I'm sorry,'
He murmurs,
And then
Moves away

To another
Time,
Another place,
After life.

Leaving

The memory
Behind
In his place

To haunt
Confuse
Frustrate

The baby, no longer tiny.

Little Miss Harpy

Oh, Mum, you've got Pikachu!
Why didn't my packet have Pikachu?

Mu-um, can I have yours?
Please, can I?
I really *have* to have it, Mum,
I really do.
I'll die if I don't, Mum.
I really will.

It's the only one I don't have, Mum.
Please, I have to have it.
Can't I have it?

Oh, don't look like that, Mum.
I really *need* it, Mum.

Mu-um *you* don't need it.
Mu-um, *you* don't want it.
Pleeeeese, Mum, pleeeese,
I really *have* to have it.

It's what I've always wanted, Mum,
All the other kids have that one, Mum,
I have to have it, Mum,
You don't collect them, Mum.

Can I have it, Mum?

Will you think about it, Mum?
Pleeeese?
Oh, good!

Have you thought about it, Mum?
Have you? 'Cos I *really* need to know.
I can't *live* without it, Mum.

Mum, please don't get angry,
But I really need it.

O-kay
I'll wait.
I'll let you think about it for a while.

Have you thought about it, Mum????

The Hated One

The day chocolate was banned,
I thought my life had come to an end,
It was one of the things I could trust,
I thought of it as a very dear friend.

So when that mean old man,
Announced to all the land,
That chocolate was no more,
That it was going to be banned

I balled up my fists into tight little knots,
And made awful faces, too,
I planned my just revenge,
Upon the devil all dressed in blue.

How dare he say that my chockies won't be
In the shops on the shelves as they should?
No man, that can't be. It's definitely not right.
What can I eat *now* to make me feel good?

No man, you won't get away with this,
This awful, terrible, horrific rule,
To ban chocolate from all of us needy folk,
What do you take me for, some kind of fool?

You wait, I'll get you, you mean old man,

I bet you're a diabetic or worse,
It won't matter to you what you're doing today,
But watch out for my witchety curse.

May your pants catch aflame,
And your hair fall about you,
May your wife turn fat and bald,
And let me wish this thing on you, too

May you not be able to live without
My favourite chocolate in your mouth.

Corners of Time

Skipping from stone to stone,
Stumbling over the broken cracks,
Reaching for weedy redemption
Amongst the corners of time.

Looking backwards over a shoulder,
Looking forwards round the bend,
Looking right into the sun,
Looking left into the shadows.

Never looking into now.

Pull the second hand,
To stop the minutes
From tumbling through the glass
Of hours wasted, unwanted.

Always believing that all is right,
Often pretending it is reality,
Sometimes wondering where you are,
Rarely playing the right game,
Never seeing the truth.

Until it is almost too late.

Monster Tub

I've a monster in my tub,
I know he's there for sure,
Although I haven't seen him,
I've heard his deep, deep roar.

He's very, very thirsty,
I've seen him drink his fill,
He sucks so very fast, you know,
As if he wants to kill.

My mum keeps on insisting,
I have nothing much to fear,
But how can I believe her,
When, loudly, all around, I hear

The growls and mighty roars
As the monster, he grows near.
I'm sure that he will get me,
If I forget to check my rear.

So I sit here in the water,
And keep twisting and keep turning,
Trying very hard to spot him,
Through the bubbles and the churning.
But I never yet have seen him,
Not once in gruesome flesh,

Not even his monster finger,
Through the open plug hole mesh.

Do you think he might be shy?
Could it all be just a show?
Like the bully at my school,
Jake MacGuire, you might know.

Jake's all noise and bluster,
He is big and he is tall,
But he's not so very tough,
If you stand and do not crawl.

Might it be my scary monster,
Is really just the same,
All noise and loud commotion,
Playing a scary monster game?

But he sucks at all my fingers,
When I pull out the rubber plug,
I'm sure that he must think me,
Some big, colourful, tasty bug.

I'm sure that there's a monster
All fierce that I should fear,
So maybe I should shower,
Maybe that will keep him clear.

As long as I keep all my toes
Well away from the shower hole,
I'll be safe while I am washing,
From the shower time sucking troll.

The Bearmaker

The Beginning

Decide upon a pattern
Sitting, standing, laying.

Choose

The fur – short, long, mohair, synthetic,
One colour, multi-coloured, tipped, dyed,
Sparse, not fur at all.

The paw pads – suede, felt, velvet, fur,
Trimmed, not trimmed.

Layout

Draw up the pattern pieces,
Make two of each piece,
Then slap them on the fabric
And trace.

Be careful to transfer all markings.

Cutting out

Carefully cut

The backing only.

Otherwise fur ends up
Everywhere
And you spend the next
Three weeks cleaning it up.

Putting together

Best to tack together
With an overstich
All pieces
Of each part
Of the bear.

Then
Either sew on machine
Or by hand.

The Head

Be extra careful
Here.
Shape the face

As you go.

Assembly

Place bolts in the joints

And assemble each piece
Being careful
To swear loudly
When they slip
In the tools.

Then Stuff – with small tufts of filling.

Sew   up the holes
With ladder stitch
Then pray that you can get
The nose
Eyes
And mouth

To work.

Use   a long needle
With tooth floss
And insert the eyes
In the desired position
Pull tight to give expression
And tie off.

Then   sew the nose
Pull it out
And spend the next
Three days
Sewing, pulling out
And re-doing

The nose

Until   you concede
The first time
Was the best
And give up.

Sew   in the mouth.

Dress the bear as desired.

And give it to a deserving friend.
Or relative.

Then
choose a pattern,
Sitting, standing, laying ...

Today's World

For thirty years
He'd rise early
Have his breakfast
And drive to work.

For thirty years
He'd sit all day
At his computer
Designing intricate systems.

For thirty years
He was loyal
At work and at home
In every way.

Then one day
He went home and said
'Well, I've got the bullet.
I go in a month.'

After thirty years
Just like that
No more rising early
And driving to work.

After thirty years

No more working hard
Going home late
Computers to swear at.

After thirty years
What is loyalty?
Because at fifty-three
Where will he work now?

And work he must
With two young kids
A wife and house to support
And food to put on the table.

It's been thirty years
Since he looked for a job
Had an interview
Sold his wares.

It's been thirty years
The world has changed
Hard work no longer counts
It's all one big sales yard.

It's been thirty years
Of gathering knowledge
And honing skills

That no-one seems to want.

But there's not much choice.
He grits his teeth,
Visits Centrelink
And soldiers on.

Beyond the Window

Beyond the second floor window,
I spy the green hills of trees and bushes,
That fade into the blue hills of distance,
Below the white, puffy pillows of the pale blue
   sky.

Beyond the second floor window,
The elegant almost nude poplars
Sway gently in the winter breeze,
As it tickles the trunks
And they sigh their little whispers of time
   forgotten.

This side of the second floor window,
In the background,
Over-dramatised poetry blares out,
Invading my consciousness,
Reaching out to tremble
Upon the empty branches,
Of the trees beyond my window.

Beyond the second floor window,
Down below,
On the black winding stream,
Flows the mechanical perambulation of humanity,
Heading everywhere at once,

Reaching nowhere I can see.

Beyond the second floor window,
The sky is painted in clouds,
With colours like water,
Pale faded from bright,
The clouds hanging below
Are puffed and crimped in greys of many shades.

Beyond the second floor window,
Foliage of green and gold,
Blends towards the distant
Oil painted blue mountains,
Behind grey white early mist.

Beyond the second floor window,
Over my right hand shoulder,
Lies the horizon shaped by city,
Brown buildings, silver antennas,
Flowing away to the cloud ridden sky.

Beyond the second floor window,
Lies the stream of the rest of my life,
Now it is time to leave here,
And go beyond the second floor window.

Inside My Mind

Inside my mind
Lies a blood red pool
Of emptiness

Spilling itself
Over the pathways
Of my memories.

It shifts and changes
Stirring havoc
In its wake.

Until there
Is nothing left
But confusion.

Or was the confusion
Always there
Hiding in the background.

Seeping into every
Thought and memory
Stored 'safely' away.

In the blood red pool
Where emptiness swallows my mind.
Is it an essential,
Unwanted,

Part of me.

Mm, or is it something new?

Something I've only
Just discovered

Here in the blood red darkness.

Oh, God, I don't know.

I wish I did.

Or, at least, I think I do.

But, then, maybe I don't.

Maybe I should just forget it.

Maybe I should just think about something else.

Maybe I should just stop asking these questions.

These questions are just too confusing.

Swirling in the emptiness
Of the blood red pool
Inside my mind.

Strange Encounter

Last week
I met the Easter Bunny.
He didn't look like
The Easter Bunny, though.
You know, as you'd imagine,
Tall, white,
Long, straight ears,
Perhaps wearing a waistcoat,
With a basket over one arm.

No, he's really grey,
Comes up to about my shoulder,
So he's not very tall at all,
And his ears hang down
To his waist.

The day I met him,
He was wearing a hoola skirt,
And a large pair of dark glasses.
Even now I can't work out
How he kept those on.

He was a nice fella, really.
We chatted about all
Sorts of things.

Amongst them, the cost
Of Extras in health insurance.

He was quite angry at how
Expensive it was,
Especially
When he only wanted it
For the dental care.

Yeah, we had a good chat.

I know it was the Easter Bunny,
Because when he left
He hopped away.
And where he'd been standing
Was a six-inch high, brightly foiled egg,
And, oh, it was the best egg I've ever tasted.
And I've tasted quite a few.

Yeah, it was definitely the Easter Bunny,
Even though, up till then,
I didn't think he existed,
And, he didn't look like what I'd imagined.
Yes, it was definitely him!

Revisiting

Crystal ball
Into the future,
Endings apparent,
Bubble of time stands still.

Hurriedly waking,
Blinking the light away,
Stumbling towards
Something incomprehensible.

The focus puller
Works overtime,
Drawing disaster closer,
Leaving all else
To drop away.

Until only fate remains.

For a second
There is darkness,
Then searing red
Puts action back again.

Action mixed with a modicum of hope.

But it's fate,

No one is home anymore,
Hope leaves to try somewhere else,
Leaving a hard rock behind.

Ambulance, police, questions,
Calmness, so much calmness,
Cleaning up the mess,
Answering neighbours' queries.

The month long day
Drags on,
People coming,
How sorry they are.

A quiet time
Filled with questions,
Why did you have to go?
What will I do now?

Tears dropping
Into hands, shaking,
With what – fear, stress,
Grief, guilt, selfishness?

They all apply.
Especially guilt.
Especially selfishness.

Grief comes later.

Thirty years pass.

The questions still unanswered.

The grief well and truly present.

The Luck of Destiny

A lucky break,
Lady luck,
A four-leaf lucky clover,
A lucky rabbit's foot.

Winning a million dollars,
A new car, a holiday,
Measures of luck
In the pools of our existence.

A fatal accident
Where only minor injuries
Are sustained.

A terminal disease
That somehow
Goes into remission.

A pregnancy that shouldn't be.
A beautiful, healthy baby
For someone to love.

Not Luck,
But destiny,
Fate,
Miracles.

Peace Regained

Deep within
I delve.

I hide.

I find
A place

Of solitude

I curl up
And listen

To the quiet.

I soak in
The atmosphere,

The peace.

I replenish
My soul

With riches.

I drink in

The stillness.

I calm.

And then I emerge,

Human again.

Invisible

The sky is blue,
Wrong!
It's green.

Earth is round,
Wrong!
It's flat.

Life's a bitch,
Wrong!
You love it.

Why won't you listen?
Wrong!
You're not talking.

Why don't you feel me?
Wrong?
You're not here.

That daffodil is yellow,
Wrong!
It's a rose.

That rose, then, is yellow,
Wrong!

It's red.

That rose is red, then.
Wrong, wrong, wrong!
It's nothing!

Insignificant
Gone
And wrong.

Life in a nutshell!

Rainbow of Life

Shades of grey
Surrounded by an aura
Of browns,
Time stretching backwards,
Life standing still.

Daylight peeks out
From behind early
Morning clouds,
At first hesitant,
But not for long.

The day bursts through,
Showering gold and orange
Upon the wonder,
Overwhelming
And filling every crack.

Welcoming the blackness,
Beckoning to the blue,
Settling towards the purple,
And allowing the red
To have its reign.

Fingers of emerald green
Shoot out and wander through,

Leaving paths of turquoise
In their wake,
And streams of ebony flow strong and fast.

The colours merge and mix
And separate again
Until haphazard spots
Are everywhere
And there is no escape.

No escape and no hiding,
The hues of life
Surround and invade,
Awakening the way
It should be.

It is terrifying,
It is welcoming,
It is right.

Spirit Guide

To my Spirit Guide:

Inside my mind
Lives a black pool
Of emptiness.

But then I call
And you're there.

Inside my heart
Lives a high peak
Of uncertainty.

But then I call
And you reassure.

Around my spirit
Lives a wall
Of confusion.

But then I call
And you explain.

The emptiness.
The uncertainty.
The confusion.

Are there
When I forget to call,
When I'm too busy
To seek you out,
When I waiver
In my belief.

When I make the time
Not to forget,
And have the courage
In my beliefs

I call
And you are there

To guide me through my life.

Waiting

Waiting

For the bus to arrive

Waiting

For the show to start

Waiting

For the kettle to boil

Waiting

For the time to be right

Waiting

For inspiration to hit

Waiting

For someone else to begin

Waiting

For something to happen

Waiting

For something to change

Waiting

For the undertaker.

The sun rises.
The sun sets.

Snowballs

At first it's hard
To form a ball of memory.
It falls apart.
It eludes even the most
Skilled of touches.
But perseverance sees
The first round ball
Of thought
Form into a memory.

It may be jagged around
The edges and a little indistinct,
But if you keep working on it,
Gradually it becomes firmer
And more definite.

It sits firmly in your hand,
Is balanced and weighty,
Then you start to grow
Excited and you throw it
Through the air, revelling
In the joy it gives you.

You become so overjoyed
You quickly make more snowball
Memories,

Until they come so quickly and
So easily you wonder why you
Had so much trouble at the
Beginning.

Finally the memories slow.
It's enough to just throw
The snowballs you have stockpiled.
It's enough to see them shatter
And spread their joy everywhere.

Snowball memories, crystallised joy.

Mystery

Unwanted violence
 Spills out
  And erodes
   Innocent lives.

Time halts,
 While cries of anguish
  Ring out
   From the report.

The slow motion
 Of existence
  Is stilled,
   It weeps for loved ones.

A nail loosens,
 Timber falls,
  A soft clatter
   In the din.

Whispers drift down from above
 As daybreak shines
  Through laughter caught in cobwebs
   On the stairs.

Booted feet march tirelessly
 Past battered lives.

Glare fires like spent time
On the breeze of black forgotten dew.

The bleached ram's horn
  Lies white inside the dawn,
    Footprints fade in the lonely breeze,
      Following the echo of voices.

Harsh cries fly
  From a distance,
    Falling on ears
      No longer hearing.

Mist clings to the landscape,
  Like phantoms of hope,
    Groping wearily
      For the last crumbs of Spring.

Life's jigsaw puzzle
  Spins out of control,
    Shooting stars leap
      Spirited away into oblivion.

At its starting point
  Mystery
    Lasts forever.

Caught Between Hope and Fear

Wondering, imagining,
Lost amidst life,
There are no clues to be found
In this palpitating awareness.

Darkness behind,
Caught - grey dim
In the sandwich
Of bright light ahead.

Wondering, amazed
At what might be,
Hesitant beyond
What has been.

Somehow paralysed
Into immobility with action,
Extremities only
Touching life with movement.

Wondering, hoping,
Caught indecisive
Beside the giant pool
Of desire.
Daring to strive
Through moments of adversity

Towards microseconds of dreams
Between lines.

Wondering yet fearful,
Hoping to dare,
Dreaming of life

As it should be.

Not caught between hope and fear.

The Funniest Thing

I spread my legs wide,
And I swung like a pro,
But the ball it just sat there,
All smuglike, you know.

Miss, one.

I swung from the right,
And followed right through,
But I just clipped the top,
And it rolled to my shoe.

Miss, two.

My face grew all red,
My hands gripped so tight,
I glued my eyes to the ball,
I was ready to fight.

Miss, three.

All about me they laughed,
And snickered and clapped,
So I drew back my club,
And swung till I snapped.

Miss, 63.

I know I was right
In the way that I played,
I stepped up to the ball,
And I fervently prayed.

Miss, 87.

I swung and I swung,
And I laughed till I cried,
My sides were all splitting,
As the game quickly died.

Miss, 173.

I rolled on the grass,
Tears streamed down my cheeks,
It was the most fun I'd had
For weeks and weeks and weeks.

When the score reached 200,
I conceded defeat,
The whole course only,
Had a par of 27 to beat.

So I sat on the side,
And watched everyone win

Their game of mini-golf,
My face wide in a big fat grin.

Accidental Knowledge

Vivid images, drawn horror,
Float in the air before my eyes,
Visions I see and could
Not ever possibly know.

Words float from a distance,
Through my consciousness,
Meaning lags somewhere behind,
Words I do not want to know.

Despair, fear, unreality,
Breach the recesses of my breast,
My heart stands still,
I wish I did not know

Endless hours of waiting,
No word to ease my pain,
Pictures invade my imagination,
Do I really want to know?

Seeing, disbelieving
That this could really happen,
It's always someone else,
Never anyone you know.

But this time I know.

Beginning

My excitement bubbles
And my fears gurgle
In the pit of my stomach.

First day jitters.
"You'll be fine,"
Says Mum

'What does she know?
She probably can't
Even remember secondary school.'

The bus is on time,
Pity!
I climb on slowly,
Grab the nearest seat,
And try to disappear.

No one takes any notice
Of me.
My disappearing act
Works.

I straighten up.
Hey, people, I'm here,
Look at me, Gracie Brown.

They keep on chatting,
Spreading their holiday
News around the bus
To everyone except me.

I don't have any friends
Here.
I know I never will.

I hate secondary school.
I hate school buses.
I hate me.

My Favourite Martian

I've a Martian in my bedroom,
He's really very cute,
Stands two feet from the floor,
And wears a Martian suit.

"Two foot from the floor?" you say,
"'Tis a most peculiar man",
Until you know his story,
Then you'll understand.

You see he really truly thinks
that he stands upon my floor,
Among my toys and special things
behind my bedroom door.

He thinks my clock works backwards,
As it ticks from 1 to 2,
But we all know that it doesn't,
At least, I do, don't you?

His ship came down one cloudy night,
When it was dark and foggy,
And he landed in the forest,
In a field that was all boggy.

He steered it wrong as he came down

And got into a muddle,
He drove it backwards through our time
Straight for a giant puddle.

When the light of day rose in the air,
He checked his spacecraft out,
He found it was beyond repair,
Of this there was no doubt.

So now he's stuck here all alone,
Living from end to start,
And we are friends, my Martian and I,
And I love him with all my heart.

Believe It or Not

It spreads
Along the veins
And arteries,
Warm and welcome.

It stomps
Upon the panic
And weakness,
Relentless and true.

It fills
The empty places
And spaces,
Rising and ebbing.

It firmly
Pursues the doubts
And cynicism,
Punishing and destroying.

It replaces
All the denials
And negatives,
Persistent and insistent.

Until the garden

Is strong,
Positive,
Determined,
Calm.

Until the path
Becomes straight and right.

Blue Bird Fly Free

I spy a little blue bird
Flitting through the trees,
He's small and quick and agile
He follows the evening breeze.

Come along, little blue bird,
Won't you rest upon my hand?
Won't you let me scratch your pretty head,
Oh, so gently while you stand?

I promise I'll love you dearly,
And treat you with all care,
So please come down and talk to me,
Don't just sit up there and stare.

The blue bird does not answer me,
Instead he flies away,
The little blue bird is not mine,
I cannot make him stay.

I watch as little blue bird,
Darts from bush to tree,
And I know with all my heart,
He only wishes to be free.

So goodbye, little blue bird,

Soon again we'll meet,
From now on I'll be looking up
Not looking at my feet.

The Mystery of the Missing Daphne

It happened not so long ago,
This tale I'm telling you,
And by the time I'm finished,
You will want to solve it, too.

So I'll start right at the top,
And tell you this strange tale,
From its beginning to its end,
Leaving out not one detail.

I used to have a daphne bush,
Quite some time ago,
And it grew and grew and grew,
Quite how I do not know.

Now, my mum, she tried and tried
To grow a daphne of her own,
But it didn't matter what she did
They'd die, so she would groan.

So that's why I bought my daphne
That did so very well,
But when we moved to Wallan,
I found I missed its fragrant smell.

So off I went, and bought two more,

But left them in their pots,
I took them out the sideway,
Where they nestled in their spots.

Alas, even though I watered them,
And gave them every care,
One of them lost all its leaves,
Which left its stem quite bare.

Came time to take them out the front,
To the bed near our front door,
I left them in their cosy pots still,
Until the clouds could rain some more.

But one, alas, it did not last,
It left this mortal earth,
And so I planted my last daphne bush
To save what it was worth.

It neither grew nor did it die
A fact I'm pleased to say,
But I went out our front door,
To find it gone one day.

So there you see the mystery
Of my missing daphne plant,
Where did my daphne go to?
Did it go for a run with a pant?

Perhaps it went on holiday,
Sick of just sitting and growing,
But until the daphne turns up again,
There's no sure way of knowing.

Or maybe one of the neighbours
Grew fed up with my black thumb,
And rescued poor little daphne
Before it became anymore glum.

Or perhaps the daphne fairy,
Took it away to mend it for me,
Maybe soon I'll go outside
And back in its spot it will be.

Or maybe daphne eating aliens
Saw a feast near my front door,
And came on down to add it
To their dwindling snack food store.

Oh, I don't know, I really don't,
And somehow I think I never will
But one thing's for sure, I'm telling you,
That daphne did not stand still.

Toothache

I reckon
That toothache
Would have to be
The worst pain
In the world.

Not only
Does it ache,
But it also shoots
When cold or hot
Even think of coming near.

And, then,
There's the cheek pain,
And the headaches,
And the loss of appetite,
Heaven forbid I could not eat.

Oh, that needle felt good.

Mistaken

Pores dripping fatigue,
Eyes barely slit,
Heart open and bare,
Mind in jigsaw.

Wherefore art thou lover?
Lying there beside me,
Your body, your mind,
But not your heart or soul.

Your eyes are empty
Gazing at the air,
As our mistakes coil
Around us and within us

Threatening to strangle
All that we are.

Seconds, minutes, hours,
Days, weeks, months, seasons,
Years
All gone, devoured by the monster.

Apathy, pride, selfishness, confusion.

Take your pick,
As monsters go,
They are all as bad as each other.
They have all been here

Tapping us on the shoulder,
Whispering in our ears,
Holding onto our shirt tails,
Preventing us from reaching

Each other.

Make of This What You Will

Floating
Amidst time,
Returning to the past
With a view
Through a window
From the future.

Smoky images
Wax into brightness,
Trying to re-alight
In their afterlife,
Fondness and richness
And truth.

Ghostly dreams
Echo old desires,
Seeming greater
Than tomorrow
Could ever be,
Greater than today has become.

At times
Unimportant,
Shades only of
Wisdom,
Slipping their shackles

To freedom.

They are everywhere,
Invading every crevice
Of time and thought,
Dominating,
Ruling,
Disguising.

Do you remember?

Magical Moment

Mix a dewdrop of happiness,
With a calm summer's day,
Stir it up well,
In the green pot of clay.

Add a measure of sunshine,
Let it sit for a while,
And then, very carefully,
Add a bright, cheery smile.

Warm it all gently,
O'er coals burning bright,
Swill it around,
So it catches alight.

It will sparkle and float,
As it cures till it's done,
Be sure not to capture,
Our potion of fun.

See - it shoots its stars skywards,
It's nearly done now,
Such a myriad of colours,
I'd love to know how.

It works with a whisper,

A light sprinkling of words,
Until, at last, in a burst.
It becomes rainbow-bright birds.

Where I'd like to Be

I'd like to be sitting
Somewhere way up high,
Maybe in the mountains,
Touching the pale blue sky.

I'd like to be sitting
In the crook of a gum,
Like a sleepy koala,
Sucking its thumb.

I'd like to be swaying,
In the breeze, like a tree,
With a rustle of leaves,
That would set my spirit free.

I'd like to be gliding
Across the light blue sky,
Watching the ant people
Bustling by.

I'd like to have dreams
Where my thoughts wander free,
Across the desert, the plains
And out across the sea.

Don't get me wrong
Where I am is okay,
But I'd love to have adventures
In my life, one day.

My Scarecrow

My scarecrow and me
Are awfully alike
He stands on the hill
I sit on my bike.

Sometimes I climb
Right up to the top
Sit at his feet
And talk non-stop.

I always have
A real lot to say
And he always listens,
Sometimes all day.

He doesn't judge me
And he doesn't shout
He seems to know
What I'm all about.

He never butts in
As I chatter away
He listens so well
To all that I say.

My scarecrow and me
Have a lot that we share
I listen to him
And I watch him stare.

I know he is lonely
And feels out of place
The birds do not fear him
They laugh in his face.

I know how he feels
To be lonely at heart
But I'll be his friend
Even when we're apart.

'Cos I don't have friends
I could count on, you see
My scarecrow and I
Are the same, him and me.

But now he and I
Can be friends to each other,
That will always be so
Even when there's another.

Haiku Trio

Blue mountains rise high
Clouds float past
Desert drowns

Brown rock moves
Another is still
Turtle meets rock

Breeze moves trees
Storm bends trees
Hurricane breaks

Wants, Needs, Wishes

I've always wanted something,
I've never been content
Just to have whatever I have
Instead of what is meant.

I always seem to need something
I'm sure it can't be so
At *some* stage my needs should be met
But I really just don't know.

If only wishes were real
I could wish my wants and needs
Then I could be happy,
With all my worldly deeds.

I'd wish for peace and happiness
For everyone I know
And all those who are strangers
Be they friends or be they foe.

With everyone happy in their lives
Perhaps the world would be as one
And wants and needs would disappear
As we all have joy and lots of fun.

No one would be hungry
And the earth would be healthy and fit
As caring became a priority
As everyone did their bit.

Imagine living with happiness
Every day whether raining or sun
Imagine loving everyone
Regardless of what they have done.

With wishes I could wish
To make everything be just right
For everyone on this earth
Every day and every night.

With no more wants and no more needs
And no more poverty at all
Everyone's wishes would come true
And we could all stand straight and tall.

Equality would be a thing so real
That no one would be unkind
And love and peace would prosper
No hardship would we find.

Too good you say and laugh I'm sure
Well maybe that is true
But we all must try to have our dreams

Or else our life is through.

So close your eyes and make your wish
Banish those wants and needs
Open your eyes tomorrow
And follow your wishes with deeds.

Reality

Ghosts of time,
Ghosts of space,
Apparitions rocketing
Through my heart.

Glaring lights,
Glaring pain,
Breath caught
Somewhere amidst time and space.

Floating mindless,
Floating blindly,
Groping for a way
To come back, to be.

Wishing for death,
Wishing for truth,
Hoping that time
Will reverse.

Wanting it all to disappear,
Wanting the air to be clean
Of all the doubts
And resentment
And bitterness.

It always happens
To someone else.

Visions of Family

Kid 1: Mum, my tummy hurts.

Mum: You ate too many lollies, that's all.

Kid 1: I feel like I'm gonna throw up.

Mum: Quick. To the toilet. Come on.
Oops, too late.

(A short time later)

Kid 2: Mum, I don't want to sit
In the back of the car,
With her.
She might throw up again.

Mum: Oh, all right,
I'll sit with her,
You can sit in the front.

(At the car)

I'm stuck, I'm stuck
Wait I can't get my foot in.
There's not enough room.

Okay, got it, off we go then.

Kids: Hooray, Hoorah,
Mum's stuck in the back of the car.

Mum: Meanies.
Thanks.
I love you, too.

(In Bunnings car park,
on the way home)

Kid 1: Mum, whe-ere's Dad?

Mum: He's in Bunnings, dear,
He won't be long,
He just had to pick up
a couple of things.

How are you feeling now?

Kid 1: Okay, Can't he get back, Mum,
I'm bored.

Mum: He won't be long, dear.

Get out of there, now, Kid 2
Get out of there, now,
You don't *need* the road directory.
Get out of there, NOW.

Kid 2: Yes I do.

Mum: No you don't
Not unless you need to know
where we're going
Not unless you're going to drive.

Kid 2: I am.
We're gonna go here,
and we're gonna go there,
And over there, too.

Mum: But your feet can't reach the pedals.

Kids: Mum, I'm bored, I'm bored,
Where's Dad?
Come on, Dad.

Mum: Sit down, be quiet.

Kid 1: Look! I opened the door,
That's just what I needed.

Mum: That's enough, sit down.

Kid 2: Bam Bam Badabam
Bam bam badabam.

Kid 1: Stop it, germ face.

Mum: Don't play with the mirror.

Kid 1: Look what you did,
You just mucked it up.

Mum: Come on, sit down,
Daddy's coming.

Kid 1: Thank you, God, for bringing Dad.

Kid 2: Oh, you're so unfunny.

Mum: Right, that's enough.
Daddy's here now.

(Grins all round.)

The Author

Pam Collings lives in Wallan Victoria with her husband, two teenage daughters, two dogs and two cats.

Her day job as an editor, proof reader, tutor and publisher keep her massively busy but she tries to spare some time for writing occasionally.

She loves to read, go to the movies, make teddy bears and play the clarinet in the local Mitchell Shire Concert Band.

Apart from poetry, Pam also likes to write fantasy novels for both young adults and adults and often there is a sprinkling of romance in there as well.

She has also dabbled with children's books both picture and chapter books – a few of which she will be publishing with TB Books in the near future.

Coming Soon

Pam Collings

Pam Collings will soon be releasing a second poetry anthology so if you enjoyed this one and would like to sample some more, contact TB Books on:

info@tbbooks.com.au

www.ingramcontent.com/pod-product-compliance
Lightning Source LLC
Chambersburg PA
CBHW050557300426
44112CB00013B/1955